Easy Piano
The Nutcracker Suite

Arranged by
Bill Boyd

ISBN 978-0-7935-2122-7

HAL•LEONARD®
CORPORATION
7777 W. BLUEMOUND RD. P.O. BOX 13819 MILWAUKEE, WI 53213

MARCH

By PETER ILLICH TCHAIKOVSKY

Moderately (in two)

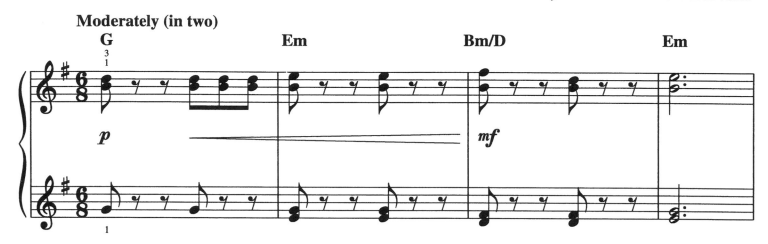

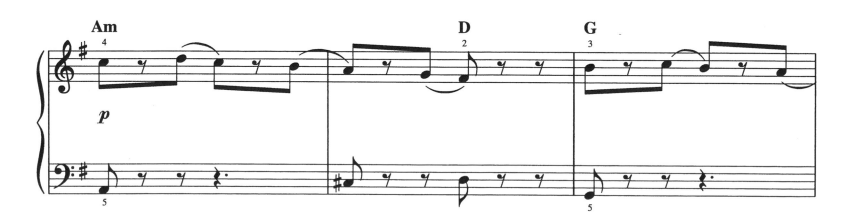

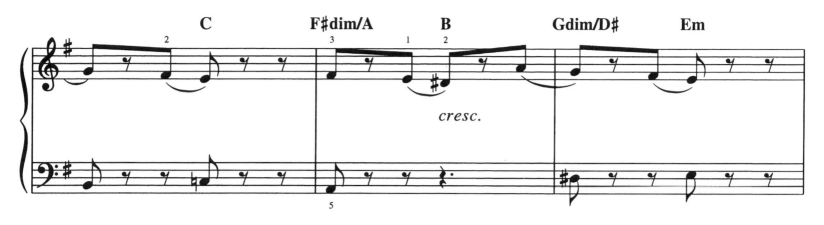

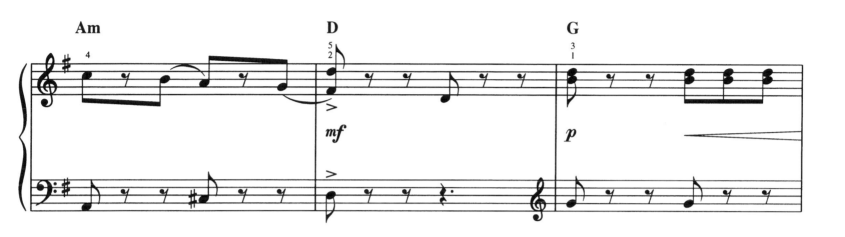

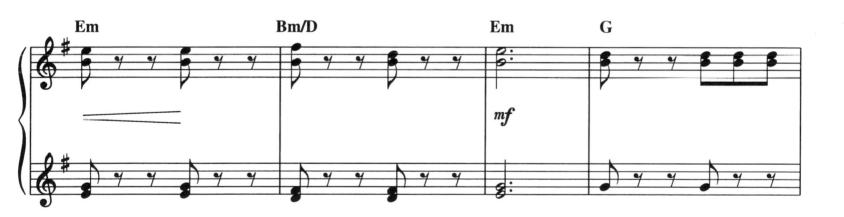

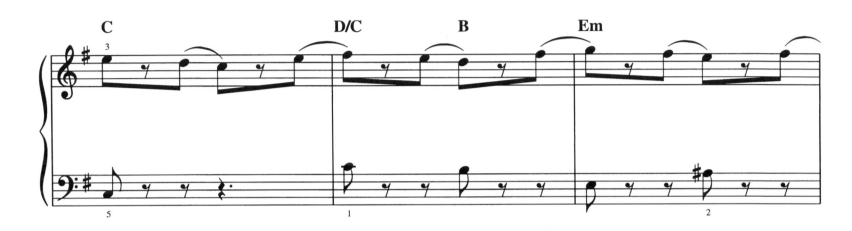

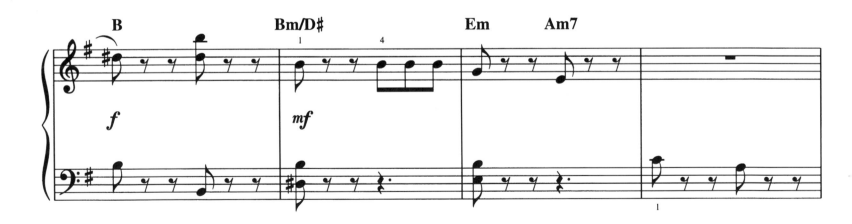

DANCE OF THE SUGAR PLUM FAIRY

By PETER ILLICH TCHAIKOVSKY

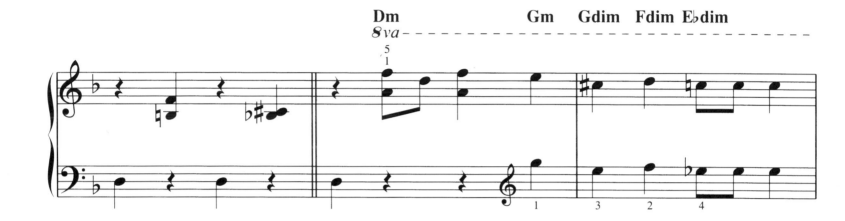

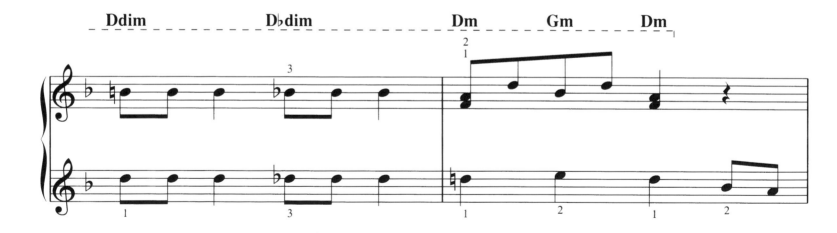

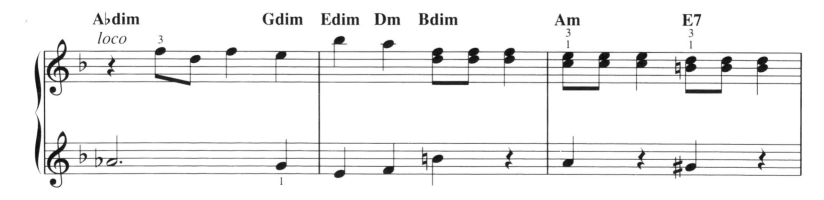

7

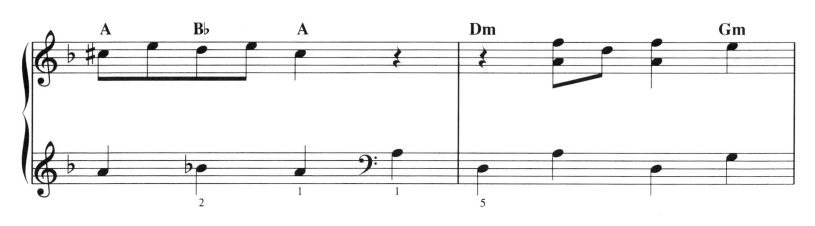

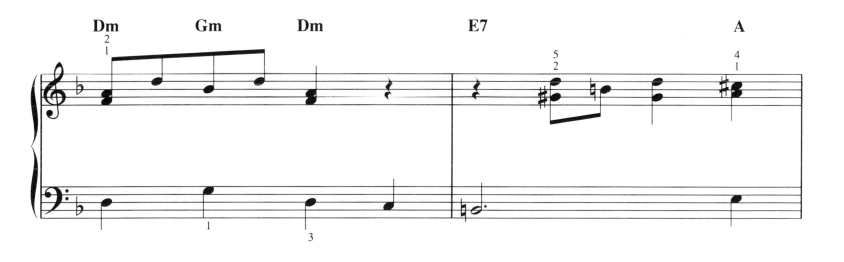

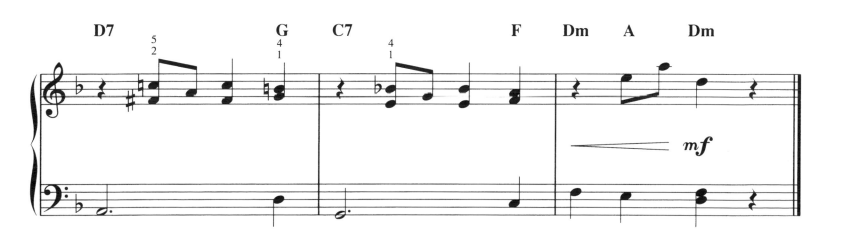

CHINESE DANCE

By PETER ILLICH TCHAIKOVSKY

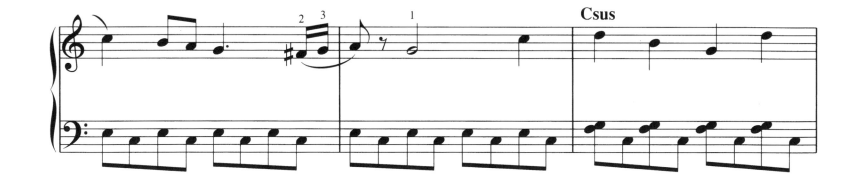

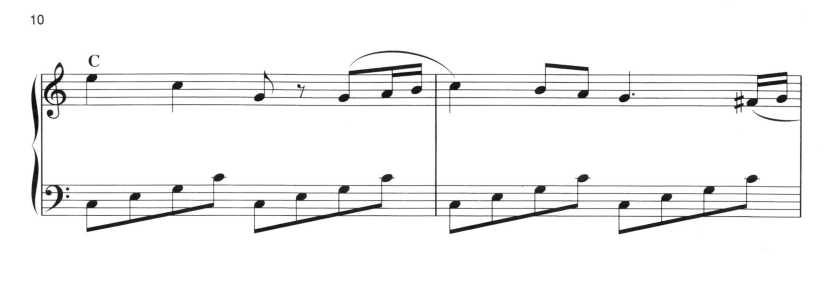

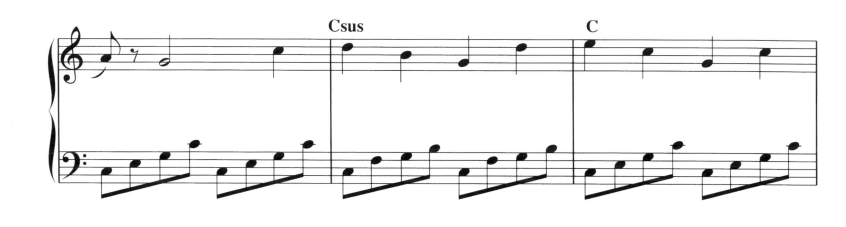

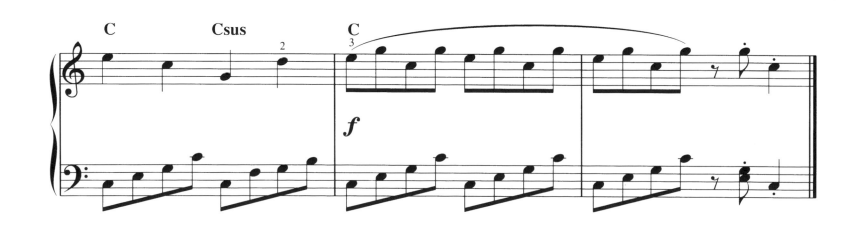

DANCE OF THE REED FLUTES

By PETER ILLICH TCHAIKOVSKY

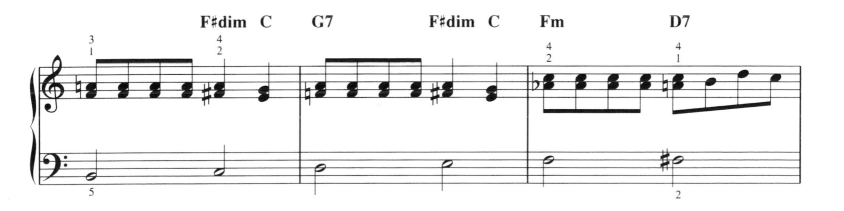

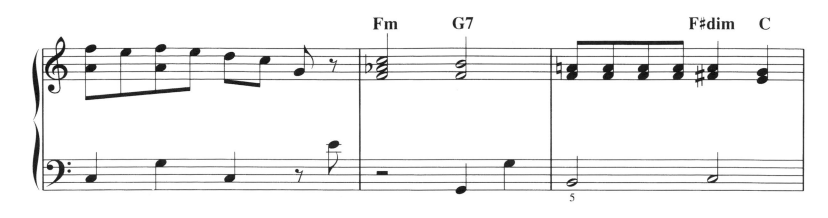

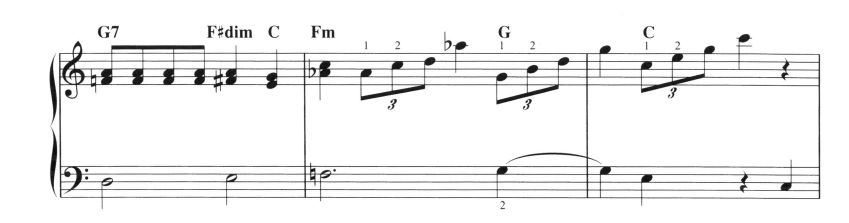

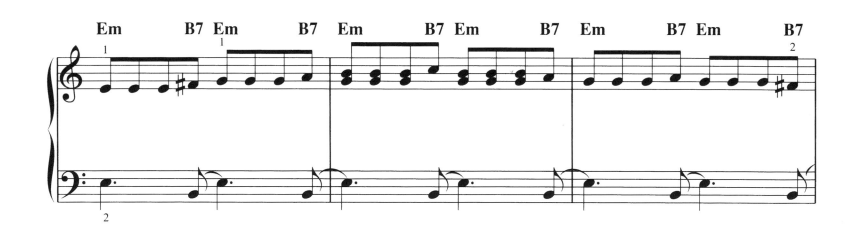

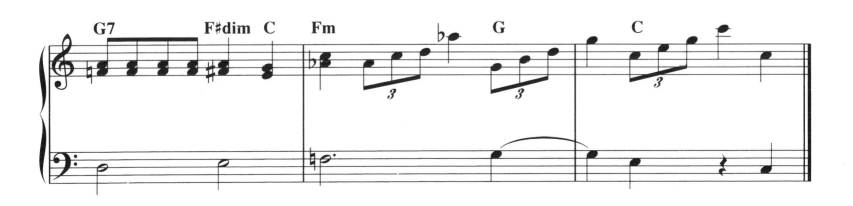

ARAB DANCE

By PETER ILLICH TCHAIKOVSKY

WALTZ OF THE FLOWERS

By PETER ILLICH TCHAIKOVSKY

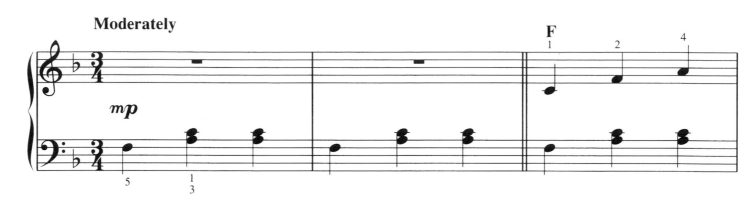

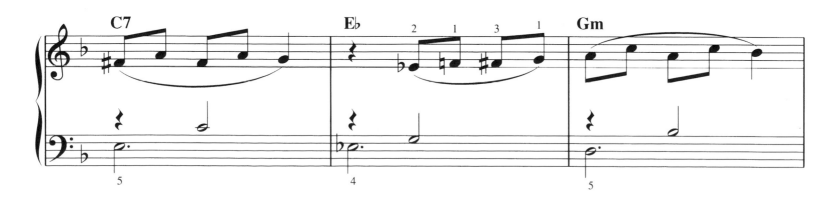

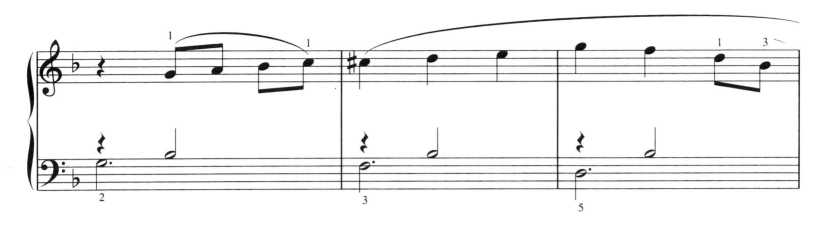

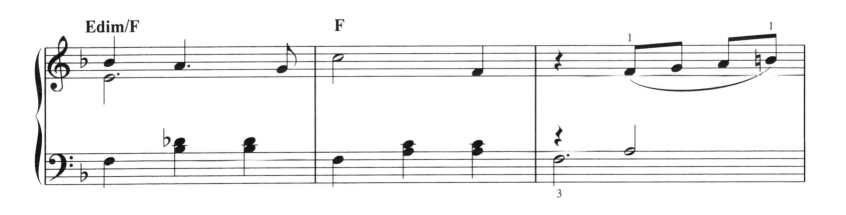

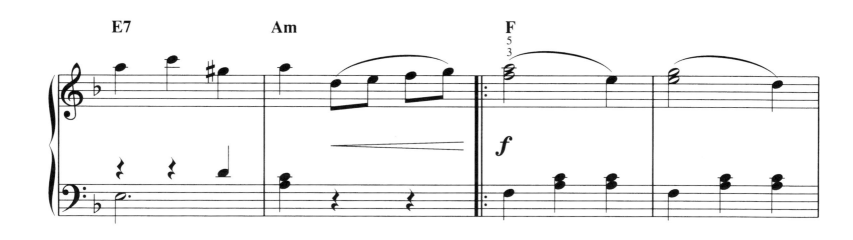

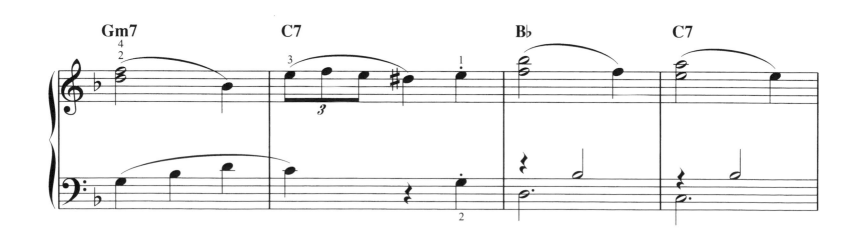

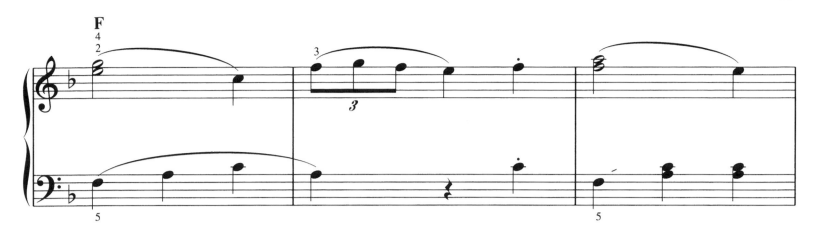

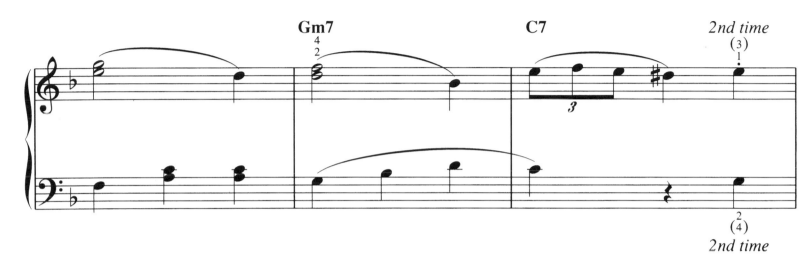

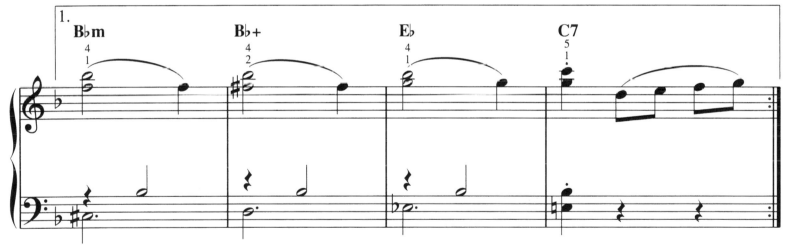

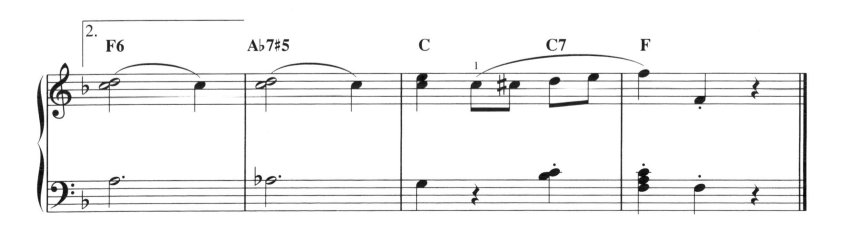

RUSSIAN DANCE

By PETER ILLICH TCHAIKOVSKY

Moderately fast

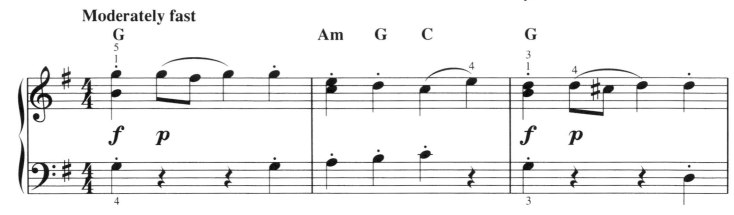

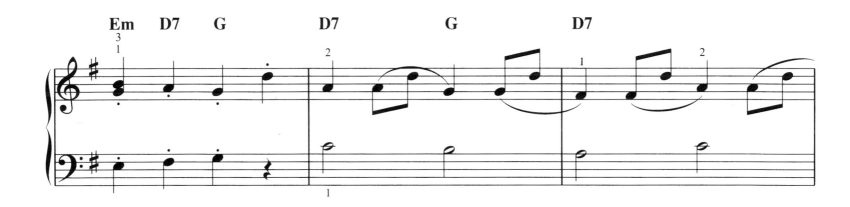

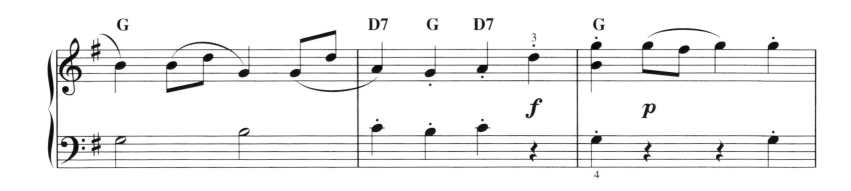

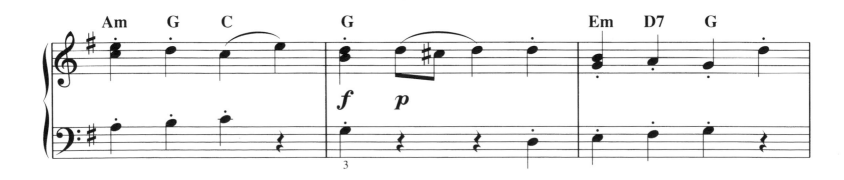

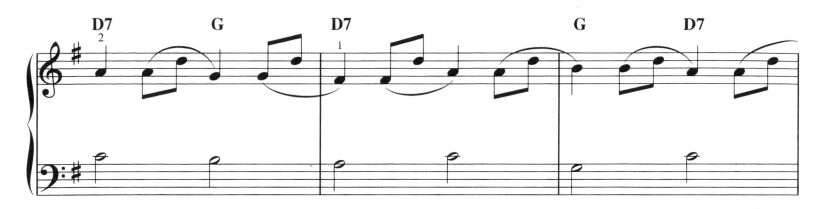

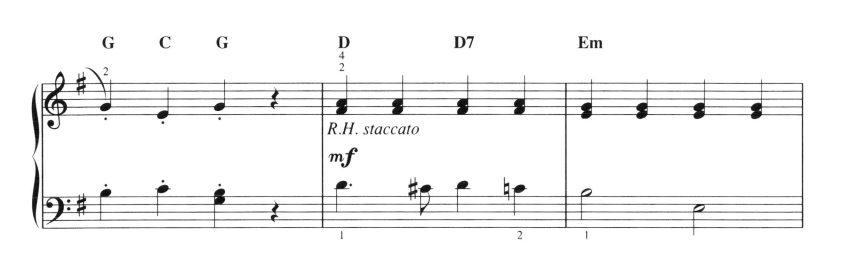

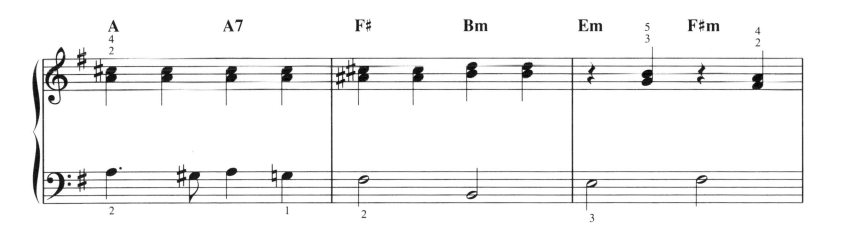

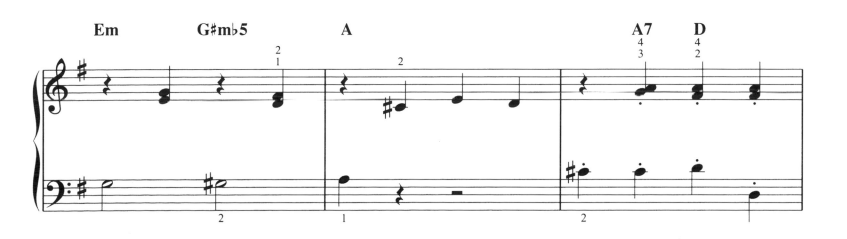